# Metal
# Embossing
## Workshop

# Metal Embossing Workshop

Magdalena S. Muldoon

Sterling Publishing Co., Inc.
New York

PROLIFIC IMPRESSIONS PRODUCTION STAFF:
Editor in Chief: Mickey Baskett
Copy Editor: Phyllis Mueller
Graphics: Dianne Miller, Karen Turpin
Styling: Lenos Key
Photography: Jerry Mucklow
Administration: Jim Baskett

Library of Congress Cataloging-in-Publication Data
Muldoon, Magdalena.
  Metal embossing workshop / Magdalena Muldoon.
        p. cm.
  Includes index.
  ISBN-13: 978-1-4027-2444-2
  ISBN-10: 1-4027-2444-6
1.  Embossing (Metal-work) 2.  Metal foils.  I. Title.

TT205.M78 2006
745.56--dc22

2005037676

2  4  6  8  10  9  7  5  3  1

Published by Sterling Publishing Co., Inc.
387 Park Avenue South, New York, NY 10016
© 2006 by Prolific Impressions, Inc.
Distributed in Canada by Sterling Publishing
c/o Canadian Manda Group, 165 Dufferin Street,
Toronto, Ontario, Canada M6K 3H6
Distributed in the United Kingdom by GMC Distribution Services,
Castle Place, 166 High Street, Lewes, East Sussex, England BN7 1XU
Distributed in Australia by Capricorn Link (Australia) Pty. Ltd.
P.O. Box 704, Windsor, NSW 2756, Australia

Printed in China
All rights reserved

Sterling ISBN-13: 978-1-4027-2444-2
ISBN-10: 1-4027-2444-6

For information about custom editions, special sales, premium and corporate purchases, please contact Sterling Special Sales Department at 800-805-5489 or specialsales@sterlingpub.com

## ACKNOWLEDGEMENTS

The projects and patterns were created by the following artists and teachers:
Alejandra Barrenechea
Paty Corella
Hortensia Dorantes
Mariluz Garrido
Deyanira Hernandez
Magdalena Muldoon
Dulce Navarro
Wendy Pimentel
Tete Pliego
Malena Porro
Cynthia Romero

I would like to thank the well-known mixed media artist, Beckah Krahula for her continuous support and advice.

# About the Artist

## MAGDALENA S. MULDOON

**Magdalena Muldoon** was born in Mexico City where she lived until 2002. Since 2002 she has lived in Dallas, Texas with her husband and three daughters.

Doing fine arts and crafts has always been a part of Magdalena's family life. Her mother, Magdalena Barrena, was passionate about gilding, book binding, and other traditional fine crafts. Because it was so hard to find a single store that had all the supplies needed for a variety of arts and crafts, Magdalena Barrena opened *Mercart* on Nov. 14, 1970, an arts & crafts store and distributor business, in Mexico City.

Around 1991, Magdalena Barrena introduced the traditional technique of metal embossing from Europe. Being the first store in the country to have the metals and tools needed to do embossing, made the success amazing. Since then, this ancient art has spread throughout the country and Latin America.

Now Magdalena Muldoon brings this craft to her current home, the United States. After learning the art of metal embossing from the best teachers in Mexico who have achieved a high level of excellence, she started teaching the art. One of the reasons she moved to the U.S. was to share all these wonderful tools, metals and the family's 14 years of expertise doing metal embossing. Magdalena shows her products at major trade shows such as *Craft & Hobby Association, Society of Decorative Painters,* and several rubber stamp and scrapbooking shows.

She also travels throughout the country giving intensive workshops and having lots of fun meeting many wonderful and creative people!

Magdalena says "I love to do metal embossing and now everything I see, just looks 'embossable'. I am happy to share this art with you."

Magdalena was taught and inspired by her mother, Magdalena Barrena. Her love of arts and crafts and expertise began developing while still a child. Today her business, *Mercart USA* sells all the tools, mediums and metals needed for the metal embossing art. Seminars are also available. You can reach Magdalena and her company at 1300 W. Walnut Hill Ln., Suite 164, Irving, TX 75038; phone 214-764-7917; fax 214-432-7494; or website www.mercartusa.com; or email at msofia@mercartusa.com.

Magdalena Muldoon shown with mom, Magdalena Barrena, who taught and inspired her.

# Table of
# Contents

# CONTENTS

# Introduction

*Metal Embossing* is an art form that has been around for centuries. Metal embossing imparts luster, radiance, intriguing dimension, and texture to metal. A variety of easy-to-use tools are used to push flat metal sheeting from the back, creating raised designs. Other equally easy-to-use tools are used on the front of the metal to refine and define the edges of the raised areas. This is the process of embossing, known as *repujado* in Spanish and *repoussage* or *repoussé* in French. A patina or antiquing medium can be applied to embossed designs to duplicate the look of age, giving the pieces an old world look.

This book explains the tools and supplies you need for metal embossing and how to use them. (Most of the education is understanding what type of mark or shape each tool makes on the metal.) The Basic Techniques section shows you, step by step, the simple procedures you need to know to create a variety of embossed metal designs. With a little practice, you'll quickly learn the amount of pressure that's required to make different types of designs.

You'll see how to create textures, make cuts in metal, finish your project, and add embellishments such as mother-of-pearl accents and cabochons. There's also information on gluing metal cutouts to surfaces, transferring patterns, and using rubber stamps, stencils, and plastic molds as sources for designs.

The third section of the book includes more than 30 projects with patterns for creating them. You'll find ideas for a variety of tabletop accessories, including boxes, trays, and napkin holders, plus frames for pictures and mirrors, wall pieces, and traditional religious icons. You'll also see how to use embossing to embellish scrapbook pages, cards, and candles.

Because of metal's intrinsic qualities of durability and permanence, when you learn the simple techniques of metal embossing you can create long-lasting treasures you'll enjoy for years to come.

# Metal Sheets

For best results, use metal sheets specifically manufactured for embossing - they have the proper gauge (thickness) and temper (the proper balance of hardness and elasticity). Metal sheeting for embossing comes in natural metallic colors - silver, copper, and brass - in rolls of various widths and in packages of cut pieces. Here are some of the characteristics of each type of metal:

**Pewter**, covered on both sides by tin - (.008 thick) Many consider tin-coated pewter, which has the beautiful shine of fine metal, to be the best metal for embossing due to its softness and manageability. It allows the tools to slide easily, achieving extraordinary dimension, volume, and movement. With the addition of a patina it gets a silver-looking antique finish. Because the pewter is coated with tin (*estaño* in Spanish, *etain* in French), the lead in the pewter does not come in contact with your hands.

**Copper** - (.005 gauge) Copper is a harder metal than pewter so you have to press harder to achieve results. Prized for its beautiful particular color, copper oxidizes to a characteristic green patina. Exposure to flame yields a variety of tones and interesting effects.

**Aluminum** - (.005 gauge) Aluminum is the least expensive metal for embossing. Because it is more rigid, its cut edges can be sharp and tools flow less smoothly. Aluminum does not tarnish. Colored aluminum - blue, green, red, gold - is also available. It's used most often for holiday-themed projects.

**Silver** - .999 pure (.004 thick) Laminated silver made exclusively for embossing is soft but more rigid than pewter. It is the most expensive metal for embossing but is highly appreciated by fine artists.

**Brass** - Because brass is extremely hard, it is difficult to work with. Its one advantage is its mellow golden color.

## CAUTIONS

- When working with metal of any type, it's a good idea to wash your hands frequently. Don't eat (or smoke) while you're working, and don't touch your mouth after you've been touching metal.
- Work in a well-ventilated area - fumes from rubber cement and other glues, lacquers, and patinas can be harmful.

# Embossing Tools

The hand tools used for embossing and texturing metal are made of metal, hard plastic, compressed paper, or wood. Most of them are mounted on shafts that resemble writing instruments, and they are used in much the same way - you write or draw with the tool on the metal, using pressure to create designs and textures or to perform tasks such as cutting.

Generally, the size of the tool for embossing should correspond to the size of the area of the design being embossed (the same way a paint brush is chosen in decorative painting to fit the size of the area you plan to paint). TIP: If the tools don't seem to flow smoothly over the metal, rub the metal with some hand lotion, wax paper, or conditioner.

## STYLUS

A stylus is used to trace designs on the front side of the metal to transfer patterns and to etch flat areas of the metal to create textures. The one in the photograph is a double-ended stylus. One end has a 1 mm ball, the other has a 1.5 mm ball.

## REFINERS

Refiners are metal tools with a curved end and a rounded tip. As their name implies, refiners are used to refine the contours of an embossed design. This tool is usually worked on the front of the metal piece. The end of the tool can be made of steel or brass, and they come in a variety of sizes. (The point of a hard plastic tool can be used for the same purpose.)

## DRY POINTS

Dry points are metal cutting tools made of hardened steel. Use a dry point for cutting intricate or curved designs and for cutouts within designs. The photograph shows dry points in two sizes, 1.5 mm and 2 mm.

## WOODEN THUMB

This handy tool, made of wood and shaped like the curve of a human thumb, is used to emboss or "puff" large areas of a design. Use it when working from the back of the metal. Unlike other embossing tools, the wooden thumb is used while you hold the metal piece in the palm of your hand.

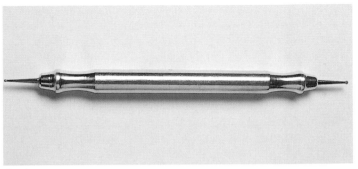

Stylus

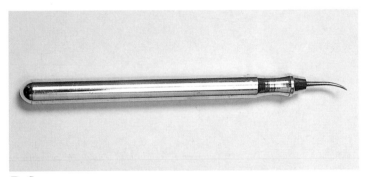

Refiner

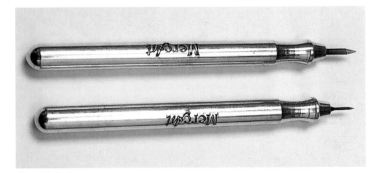

Dry Points

Wooden Thumb

## PLASTIC EMBOSSING TOOLS

Plastic embossing tools have hard plastic (typically Teflon®) tips in a variety of shapes - rounded, beveled, chisel, pointed, and deerfoot. The shafts can be wood or metal, and the tools may have one shaped tip or two.

The tools with pointed, chisel, and beveled ends are used to refine and smooth the front of the metal around the embossed areas of the design. The tool with a pointed end can also be used to define the inner edges of embossed designs, to emboss fine lines and details, and for writing on metal. The deerfoot tool is mainly used to flatten (on the front) the metal. The tools with rounded tips are used for embossing the back of the metal piece.

## BRASS & STEEL BRUSHES

Brass brushes look like stencil brushes or paint brushes but they have metal bristles. They are used for adding texture on metal surfaces - they produce a matte finish - and can be single- or double-ended. When you use them, you work on the front side of the metal.

## PAPER STUMPS

Paper stumps are compressed paper tools with pointed ends - they look like sharpened pencils - that come in a variety of sizes. They are used for embossing (particularly when creating designs with plastic molds or stencils), to soften areas embossed with tools that have harder tips (such as hard plastic and metal), to flatten areas of raised relief, and for pressing and burnishing when making repairing tears. Use them when working on the back of the metal.

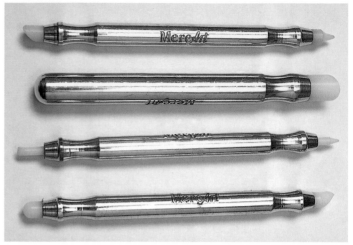

Plastic Embossing Tools

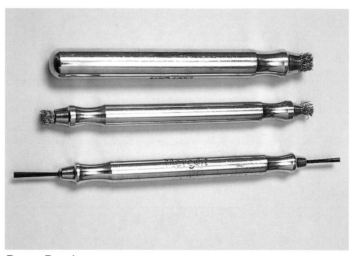

Brass Brushes

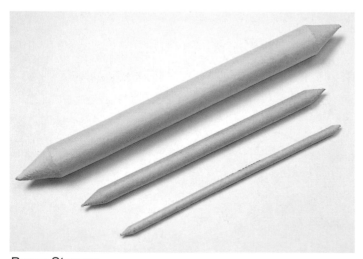

Paper Stumps

## SAMPLER OF TEXTURES
*Pictured on page 13*

**Row 1:** (Square 1) Decorating wheel with horizontal pattern from front on suede; (2) Various sizes of cups and balls, dots with point of refiner, from front on suede; (3) Front is scratched with brass brush (4) Loose thread pattern with stylus from front, no suede; (5) Tiny squares made with stylus or refiner from front, no suede; (6) Diagonal with gap pattern decorating wheel from front on suede.
**Row 2:** (1)Morse code decorating wheel from front on suede; (2) Squares and diagonal lines within squares with stylus, no suede. Ruler recommended; (3) Parallel lines made with pointed plastic embossing tool, from back on suede. On front without the suede, one side of the line was defined with the same plastic tool. On the front without suede, make diagonal lines with same plastic tool; (4) Several sizes of cups and balls were used. The ball is used from the back on suede and the cup is used to refine or clean from the front without suede; (5) Stylus used from front on suede to draw the stones. Paper

# SAMPLER OF TEXTURES

This sampler is done with a variety of the tools to show some of the textures
and backgrounds that are possible.

**The rows are listed top to bottom. The squares are listed left to right.**

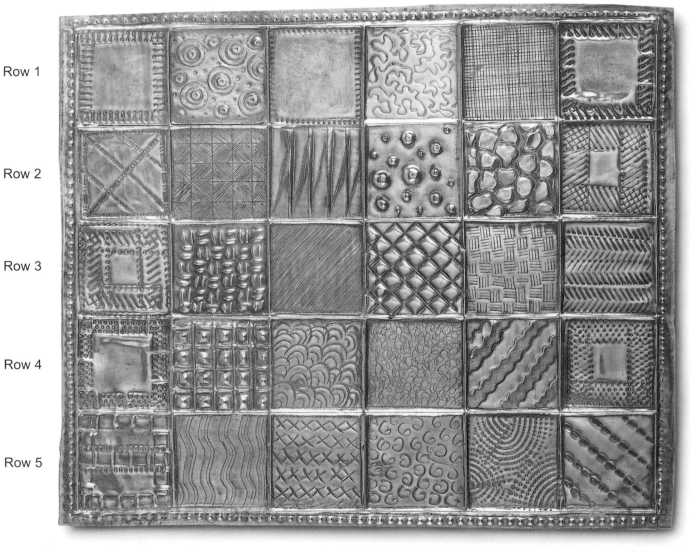

Row 1

Row 2

Row 3

Row 4

Row 5

stump is used from back on suede to emboss each stone. With pointed plastic tool, front is refined, without suede; (6) Wide diagonal decorating wheel from front on suede.

**Row 3:** Triple decorating wheel from front on suede; (2) Stylus used to make basket weave pattern from back on suede; (3) Microwheel used to scratch pattern. Don't press hard or wheel won't roll; (4) Stylus used from front on suede, ruler recommended; (5) Stylus or refiner used from front without suede; (6) Herringbone decorating wheel from front on suede

**Row 4:** (1) Points with gap decorating wheel from front on suede; (2) Stylus used from back on suede to make lines/squares. Paper stump used on back to emboss each square. A stylus or cup and ball #1 used to make a dot in the center of each from back on suede; (3) Stylus used from front

on suede; (4) Stylus from front no suede; (5) Stylus used with suede to draw wavy lines, one from front, the next from back; (6) Wide points decorating wheel.

**Row 5:** (1) Squares decorating wheel and squares with stars decorating wheel from front on suede; (2) Saw teeth brass brush used to make wavy lines from front on suede; (3) Stylus from front no suede; (4) Stylus used from front on suede to make "G" and "6" designs; (5) Star decorating wheel from front no suede, go back and forth while turning the metal; (6) Dash-space decorating wheel from front on suede.

*Note: For years this basic sampler has been used as a finished project. Hopefully you will be inspired to do one.*

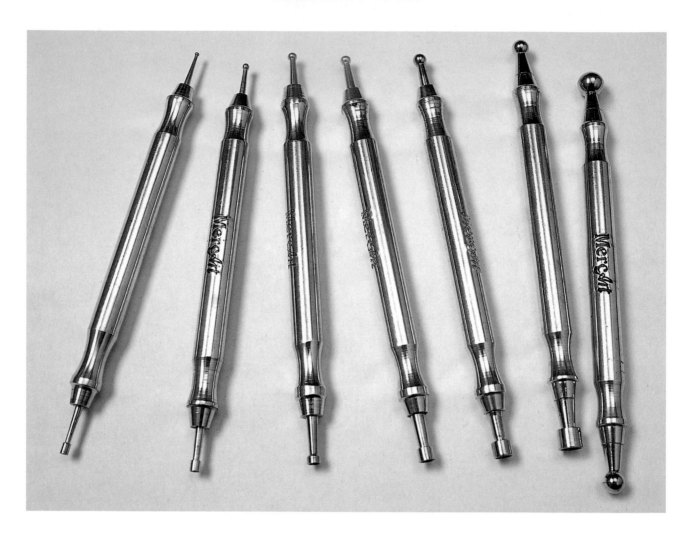

## CUP AND BALL TOOLS
*Pictured above*

Cup and ball tools are used for making a variety of textures. They have a cylinder shape with an indented ball shape on the end - the cup - on one end and a ball shape on the other end. They come in a variety of sizes. Use the ball end when shaping dimensional dot designs on the back of the metal and the cup end for refining the edge of the dot on the front. The ball end also can be used for embossing rounded shapes.

## DECORATING WHEEL SAMPLER
*Pictured on page 15*

**Section A:** (listed from top to bottom) The designs were made from the front of the metal on suede. (1) Points wide wheel; (2) Points narrow wheel; (3) Points with gap wheel; (4) Diagonal wide wheel; (5) Diagonal narrow wheel; (6) Diagonal with gap wheel; (7) Horizontal narrow wheel; (8) Triple diagonal with dots; (9) Herringbone; (10) Herringbone with gap; (11) Big dots wheel; (12) Star wheel; (13) Dash-space wheel; (14) Dots-space wheel; (15) Morse code wheel; (16) Squares wheel.

**Section B:** These use all the same wheels but the wheels were used from the back of the metal on suede.

**Section C:** (listed from left to right) (1) Microwheel used on front no suede; (2) Diagonal with gap wheel from front on suede, lines on each side with stylus from back on suede; (3) Points with gap decorating wheel with lines made on each side with stylus, all from front on suede; (4) Dash decorating wheel with Morse code wheel on each side, done from back with suede; (5) Big dots wheel with two lines on each side, from back with suede; (6) Squares wheel in center with stars wheel on each side, from back on suede.

**Section D:** The dots on the right side of the section are made with cup and balls tool from #1 to #6.

# DECORATING WHEEL SAMPLER

All the designs in sections A, B and C were made with decorating wheels.

*See page 14 for description*

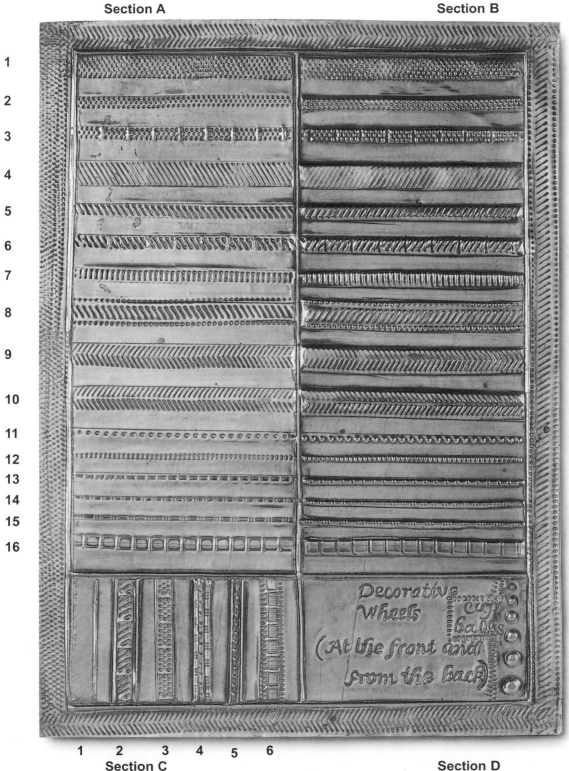

# DECORATING WHEELS

Decorating wheels are tools with roller ends that are used to make textures. Because the roller allows you to make spaced, repetitive designs, they are often used for making borders. They can also be used to add textures to flat areas of a design. To create a slight impression, place the metal, front side up, on an acrylic glass piece. For a deeper impression, place the metal, front side up, on a piece of suede.

After an embossed metal cutout has been glued to a hard surface, you can use a wheel - holding it straight up and down or at an angle as you roll it along the edge of the metal - to create a finished edge and provide additional pressure for firm adhesion.

The wheels can also be used with polymer clay, paper clay, and cardstock.

Using a decorating wheel

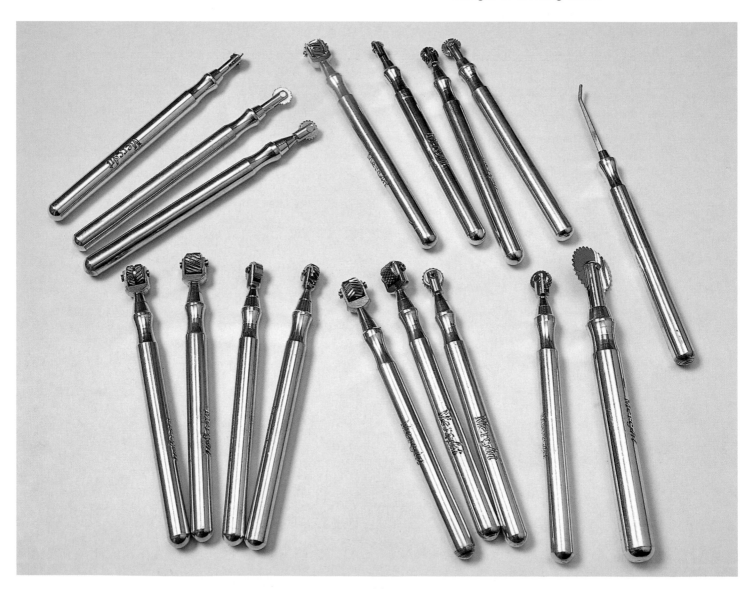

# DECORATING WHEEL SAMPLER

Textures created with decorating wheels

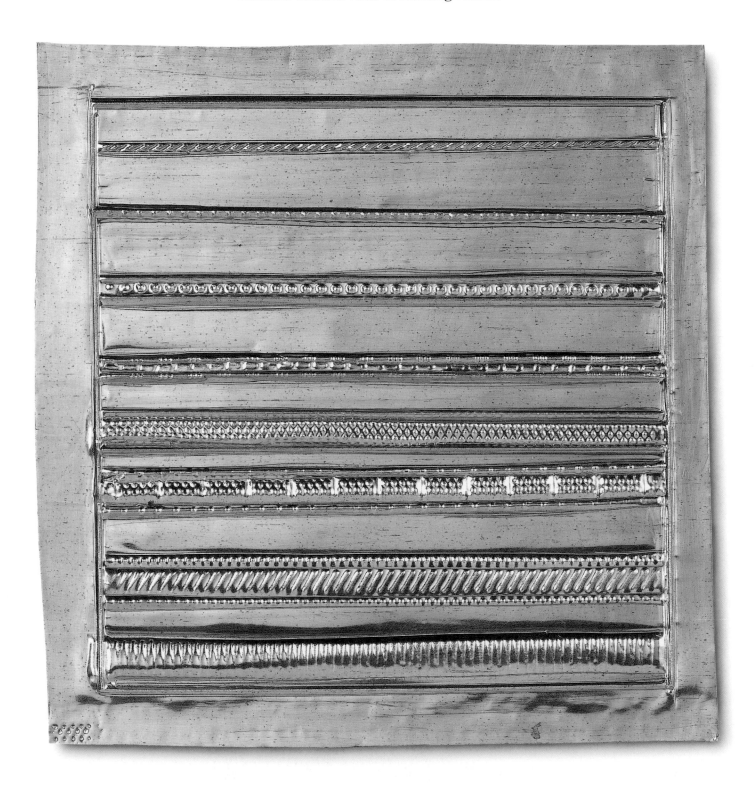

## PLASTIC MOLDS

Plastic molds are used for creating textures. Use them to create borders around embossed motifs or for making embossed panels. A paper stump is used to push the metal strip into the mold to create texture. A hard plastic tool is used to further deepen the embossing.

Plastic molds shown with a plastic embossing tool
and a paper stump.

## SAMPLER

This sampler was done with a variety of decorating wheels from front of metal on suede. It is so beautiful it could be used as a project.

# Mediums

## FILLER PASTE

An acrylic paste is used to fill the cavities on the back of an embossed piece so the piece will hold its embossed shape. The paste is soft and malleable when applied but dries firm.

Use a spatula to apply the paste, pressing firmly so it fills all the cavities of the embossing, then tap with your finger to remove any air bubbles and let dry. Remove unwanted paste from the flat parts of the metal with a damp cloth (if the paste hasn't dried) or by sanding (if it has dried.) TIP: If the paste has started to dry out in the jar, add some tap water (a little at a time) and mix well.

Before the development of this acrylic paste, a mixture of beeswax and resin melted over heat was traditionally used as a filler. It can soften or melt if exposed to hot weather. Plaster mixtures are not recommended as they will crumble when dry.

## PATINA

Many metals acquire a patina over time as the result of the oxidation process, which is initiated by exposure to air and the elements. Patinas are finishes that, by the process of a chemical reaction or simply the addition of color, create the look of age. The patina you use depends on the type of metal.

**On tin-coated pewter:** Clean the surface with rubbing alcohol to remove any oil or dirt. Apply a patina product made for tin with a bristle brush all over your project. Wipe away the excess with a paper towel. Immediately apply the polish paste and rub until the desired "antique" look is achieved.

**On copper:** Apply a patina product made for copper by brushing or

*Pictured left to right:* transparent paint, transparent dye, patina, filler paste

sponging. Wipe away the excess. Let it dry.

**On aluminum:** Use black oil-based enamel paint or black acrylic craft paint as a patina. Brush over the surface, then wipe away the excess with a paper towel. Let dry.

## COLORS & DYES

You can add colors to metal by applying transparent **alcohol-based inks and dyes or solvent-based markers.** Antiquing medium can also be used. To create a stained glass effect use **transparent paints for faux stained glass.**

A product called *Betun de Judea* can be used to add golden accents to tin-coated pewter.

## POLISH

**Metal polishing paste** can enhance the shine of metal. If you have used a patina, apply the polishing paste immediately after the patina has dried. Use your fingers or a cotton ball to apply the polishing paste. Rub with a cotton cloth until the desired amount of shine is achieved.

You can also use **metal wipes** to polish the metal after patina has been applied.

# Miscellaneous Supplies

You will need these items for all your embossing projects. Have these tools on hand for each and every project you create.

## WORK SURFACE

- **Covering material** is needed to protect your work surface, such as brown paper, cardboard, posterboard, or a large cloth. Metal can scratch tabletops, they need to be protected.

- **Acrylic plastic glass piece** that is larger than your pattern design is used as a hard work surface. The metal sheet is placed on this work surface when you are working from the front of the metal piece. The firmness of the acrylic sheet allows you to smooth the metal and refine the edges of embossed areas.

## SUEDE

A piece of suede or chamois leather that is larger than the pattern design is needed. The piece of metal is placed on this for the part of the embossing process when you are working from the back of the metal to achieve dimension. The cushioning properties of the suede allow you to push and shape the metal to emboss the design. **Do not** use the suede piece when working on the front of the metal to refine the contours of the embossed areas, when flattening bumps in the metal, or when finishing areas of flat high level designs. The suede piece can be used under the metal when using decorative wheels to add texture. The texture will be deeper than it would be if you worked on a firm surface.

## CUTTING TOOLS

- **Scissors**, for cutting metal.
- **Self-healing cutting mat**, to use when cutting metal or other materials.

## OTHER TOOLS & SUPPLIES

- **Brayer**, for smoothing the metal sheet before embossing.
- **Metal repair tape**, for correcting small tears or punctures in the metal.
- **Plastic spatula**, for spreading the filler paste.
- **Rubber cement or heavy duty glue**, for gluing embossed pieces to surfaces.
- **Tracing paper**, for tracing patterns.
- **Rubbing alcohol**, for cleaning metal.
- **Metal ruler or straight edge**, to use as a guide when makes straight lines.
- **Brushes**, for applying patina.
- **Cotton cloth**, for polishing.
- **Paper towels**, for clean up.
- **Masking tape**, for pattern placement.
- **Lacquer**, for protecting the finished metal surface.

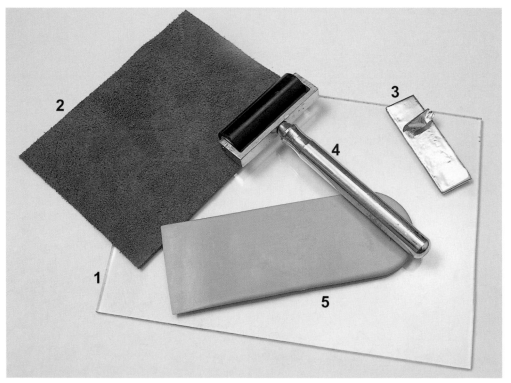

*Pictured above:* 1) Plastic glass piece, 2) suede piece, 3) repair tape, 4) brayer, 5) spreader or spatula

# BASIC TECHNIQUES

Basically, the embossing process involves using tools on the back side of the metal inside the design to create raised areas and using tools on the front side of the metal outside the design to refine and define the raised areas. This section introduces the techniques for creating the basic types of embossing - linework, curving designs, and high level flat relief.

You'll also see how to create textures, make cuts in metal, finish your project, and add embellishments such as mother-of-pearl accents and cabochons.

There's also information on gluing metal cutouts to surfaces, transferring patterns, and using rubber stamps, stencils, and plastic molds as sources for designs.

# Preparation

1. Choose a work area large enough to hold the piece of metal for your chosen project and your tools and supplies. Protect your work surface by covering it with a piece of brown paper, cardboard, or posterboard, or with a cloth.
2. Trace pattern that you wish to use onto tracing paper.
3. Using scissors, cut a piece of metal slightly larger than the pattern for your design.
4. Assemble the tools and miscellaneous supplies you'll need. (See the list of Miscellaneous Supplies on the facing page.)
5. Place the acrylic glass piece on your work surface.

---

### "PERFILES"

In Spanish, the term "perfiles" refers to the techniques of embossing lines (straight or curved) to make a design. There are two types of "perfiles." 1) Double "perfil" is any line that is cleaned or refined at both sides. The refining is done on the front of the design after it is embossed from the back. 2) Simple "perfil" is just cleaned at one side, usually the outside of the embossed line. Cleaning and refining the lines with the refiner or pointy plastic tool results in a well-defined profile.

# Embossing Linework Designs

Typically, linework techniques are used to create geometric designs and borders. Using a straight edge to guide the embossing tools ensures perfect lines. This photo sequence shows how to create embossed linework designs, step by step. The embossed panel on the top of the Celtic Knot Box, *pictured on opposite page* is used as an example.

1. **Smooth the metal.** Place the cut metal piece on your plastic glass piece. Use a brayer to smooth the metal.
2. **Transfer the design.** Place the tracing paper pattern over the metal. Tape in place. Trace over the pattern with a stylus. Remove the pattern. (The side with the transferred design is now the front.)
3. **Emboss the lines.** Place the suede piece on the plastic glass work surface, then place the metal piece, front side down, on the suede. Begin embossing the lines, using the curved back of a refiner tool and a straight edge (like this metal ruler) as a guide.

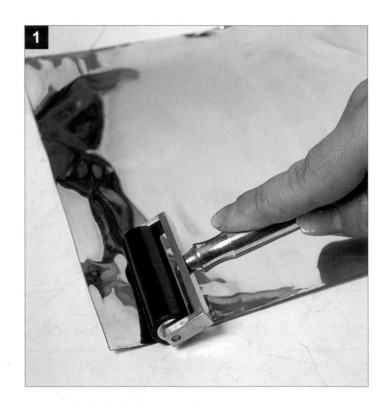

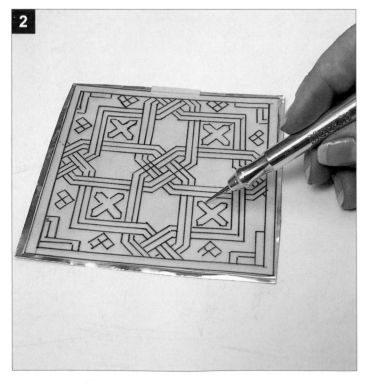

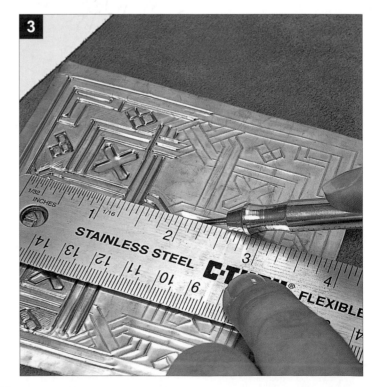

*Embossing Linework Designs, continued*

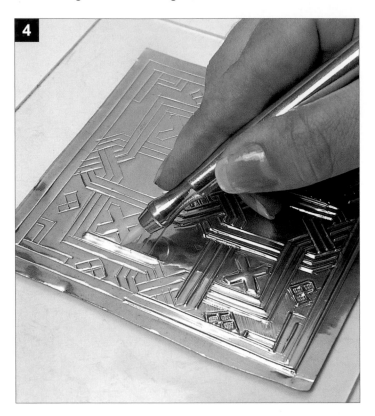

4. **Clean up the linework.** Remove the suede piece. Place the metal piece, front side up, on the plastic glass piece. Using the point of a hard plastic embossing tool, clean up the edges of the embossed design by moving the point of the tool along the edge of the linework to smooth the metal next to the linework and to refine the linework. Refining gives definition to the linework and makes the embossing stand out.

5. **Emboss other areas.** Replace the suede and turn over the metal piece so the back side is up. Use a paper stump to push (emboss) all other raised areas of the design.

6. **Define the edges of the embossed areas.** Still working on the back side, define the inside edges of the embossed areas with the hard plastic embossing tool.

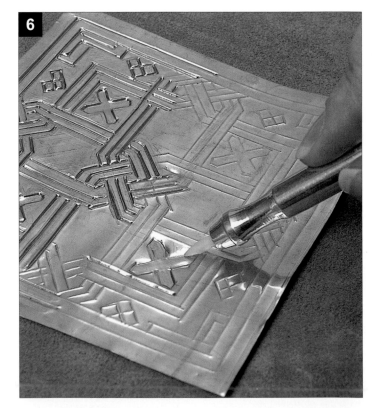

*Embossing Linework Designs, continued*

7. **Smooth the embossed areas.** Remove suede and place the metal piece, back side up, on the plastic glass. Use the paper stump to push the metal inside the embossed areas, smoothing them to create a uniform appearance.

8. **Refine the edges.** Turn the metal piece so the front side is up. Use the point of the hard plastic tool along the outside edges of the embossed areas to clean up and refine the edges.

9. **Continue refining.** Here, the same tool refines another area of the design.

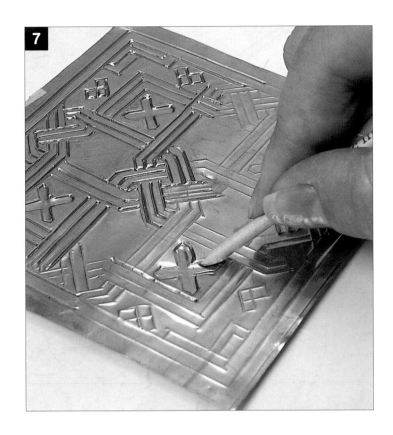

*Embossing Linework Designs, continued*

10. **Add texture.** Use the point of a refiner to create textures on the flat surfaces on the front - you want to "scratch" or "etch" the metal surface, not dent it. When adding texture, work on the front of the metal piece, and place the metal on the plastic glass piece, not on the suede. Here, parallel lines are etched into the surface on the flat areas of the design.

11. **Apply filler paste.** Apply paste to the back of the design so the paste fills the embossed areas. Spread and smooth the paste with a plastic spatula. Let dry at least 30 minutes.

12. **Apply patina.** Applied to the front side of the metal, a liquid patina medium enhances the dimension of the embossing and gives a finished, aged look to the metal. Before applying the patina, clean the surface with rubbing alcohol to remove any oils from your hands that may be on the metal. Apply the patina medium with a brush, covering the entire surface.

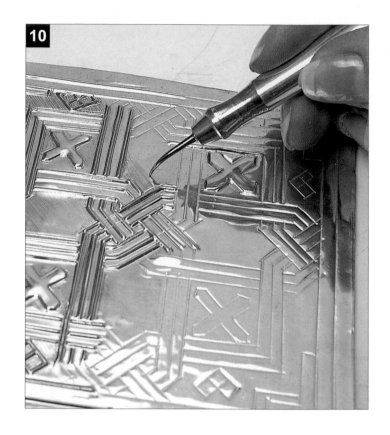

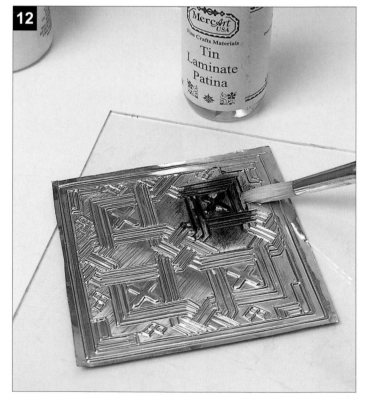

*Embossing Linework Designs, continued*

13. **Wipe.** Immediately wipe off the excess patina with a soft cloth. (You can re-apply the patina if you wipe off too much.) Immediately apply the polish.

14. **Polish.** Using a metal polish and a cotton ball, apply polish to the front of the piece. Allow to dry.

15. **Buff.** Shine the metal by rubbing with a soft cloth until the desired effect is achieved. The patina will remain in the recessed parts of the design, but not on the raised, embossed areas.

# PATTERN FOR CELTIC KNOT BOX
Project pictured on page 23.

# PATTERN FOR MONOGRAMMED SCISSORS HOLDER
Project pictured on page 31.

# Embossing Curving Designs

Curving areas of designs are embossed with round-tip tools, such as the ball ends of cup and ball tools, and the curved-edge wooden thumb tool. This photo sequence shows how to create curving embossed designs, step by step. The embossed panel on the front of the Monogrammed Scissors Holder, *pictured on opposite page* is used as an example.

1. **Begin embossing.** Working on the suede piece with the back side up, use the ball end of a cup and ball tool to emboss the flowing, curved areas of the design.

2. **Refine.** Remove the suede and turn over the metal piece. With the front up, use the hard plastic tool to refine the design, pulling the point of the tool along the outer edges of the embossed areas to define the embossing and smooth the metal beside the design.

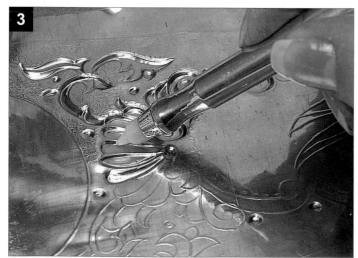

3. **Outline.** Here, the point of a hard plastic tool is used to outline areas of the design to create the illusion of overlapping. This is done on the back of the piece, working on the suede.

4. **Continue embossing.** Cup and ball tools with smaller balls are used to emboss smaller design areas.

*Embossing Curving Designs, continued*

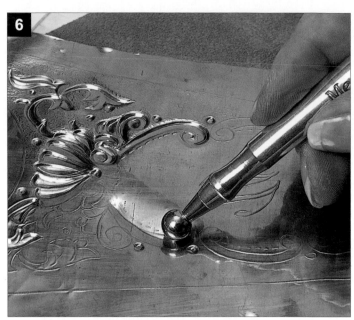

5. **Smooth.** On the front, working on acrylic piece, use the deerfoot tip of a hard plastic tool to smooth the metal around the embossed area.

6. **Continue embossing.** Here, an even larger cup and ball tool or a double ball is used to emboss larger curved areas of the design.

7. **Emboss the scrolls.** Choose the ball and cup tool with the proper size ball tip to fit the area on which you are working. Here, an intermediate size ball is used on the scroll area.

8. **Refine.** After embossing an area on the back with the ball ends of the cup and ball tools, use a hard plastic tool on the front to clean and refine the embossing. When you work on the front side, always work on the acrylic piece or a hard surface, not the suede. Working on the suede to refine the front would create "waves" on the metal.

*Embossing Curving Designs, continued*

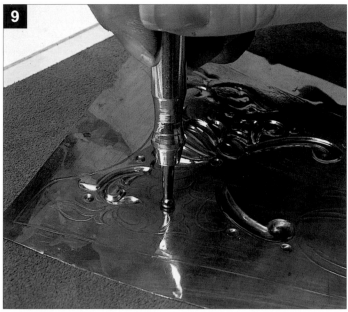

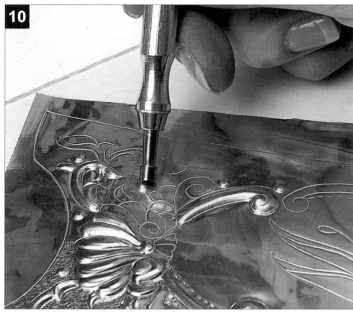

9. **Emboss the dots.** Use the ball end of a cup and ball tool to emboss the dots. Place the metal on the suede and work on the back of the metal when embossing.

10. **Define the dots.** Working on the front of the metal, on the acrylic glass piece, use the cup end of the same tool to define the dot. Here, it's pressed over the dot that was made in the previous step.

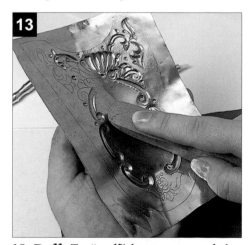

11. **Refine the dots.** Still on the front, on the acrylic glass sheet, use the deerfoot end of the hard plastic tool to smooth and flatten the metal around the dot.

12. **Etch the background.** Use the point of a refiner to etch the flat areas of the metal. Here, little squiggles fill the space around the embossed design.

13. **Puff.** To "puff" large areas of the design, hold the metal piece, back side up, in the palm of one hand and gently rub with the wooden thumb tool to push the metal from the back. Afterwards, place the metal, front side up, on the acrylic glass piece and flatten the metal surrounding the puffed area with a flat or deerfoot hard plastic tool.

*Lettering Tip:* You can write or letter (freehand or using computer fonts) using the plastic refiner tool. You don't need to do a mirror image of the letter. Just trace them lightly onto the metal and emboss them from the back with the metal on the suede.

# High Level Flat Designs

This embossing technique creates raised flat dimension or volume. It is ideal for creating designs with wide straight lines and is an effective contrast to curving dimensional designs. This photo sequence shows how to create high level flat designs, step by step. The Curving Leaves Picture Frame *pictured on opposite page* with its raised flat channel on two sides, is used as an example.

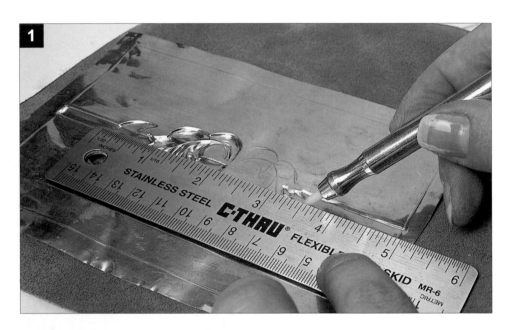

1. **Re-trace the pattern lines.** Working on the back of the metal on the suede piece, begin embossing by re-tracing the pattern lines in the area where you wish to create the high level flat design with the pointed end of a hard plastic tool. Use a straight edge ruler to guide the tool.

2. **Emboss the channel.** Still working on the back of the metal on the suede piece, use a paper stump to *gently* push the metal inside the area you have outlined, embossing a flat channel.

*Continued on page 36*

*High-Level Flat Designs, continued*

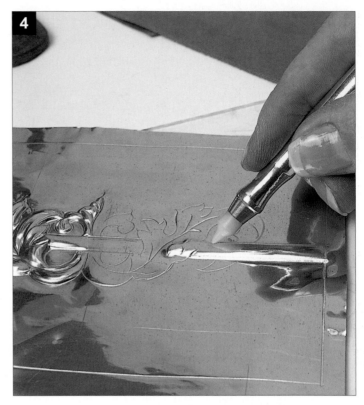

3. **Complete the channel.** Remove the suede. Working on the acrylic glass piece, *still on the back* of the metal, use the point of a hard plastic tool to press the edges of embossed flat area, and then use the paper stump or the flat surface of a hard plastic tool to again push the metal inside the channel. This creates the raised, uniformly flat area.

4. **Refine the outer edges.** Turn over the metal piece so it is front side up on the acrylic glass piece. Use the pointed end of the hard plastic tool to refine the outer edges of the embossed flat area. Flatten any bumps outside the embossed area with the deerfoot hard plastic tool.

5. **Refine the inner edges.** Turn over the metal piece so the back side is up. Working on acrylic glass piece, use the pointed end of the hard plastic tool to refine the inner edges of the embossed flat area.

*Note: The "Flat" technique is widely used in geometrical designs, ribbons, and monograms.*

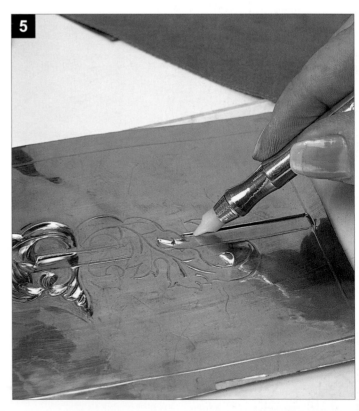

PATTERN FOR CURVING
LEAVES PICTURE FRAME
Pictured on page 35

Enlarge to 125%
for actual size

# Surface Texturing

Surface texturing can enhance a project by filling "blank" areas of a design, eliminate the bright look of flat metal, and create indentions where patina can adhere. You can do the background using any of the ideas shown on the sampler in the Tools & Supplies section or create one of your own.

Common methods of surface texturing include squiggles or fine lines done with the point of a refiner or a stylus on the front of the metal. (See the photo series on Curving Designs for an example.) You can also use decorating wheels or brass brushes to add texture to surfaces.

When creating surface textures, place the metal on the acrylic glass surface and work on the front side of the metal piece.

1. **Making tiny scratches with a micro decorating wheel.** This tool can also be used for shading leaves and flowers, or shading fabric – such as in the robes of icons.

2. **Rubbing with a brass brush to create a matte finish.** You can alter the look by using more or less pressure or by how you move the brush (back and forth, in circles or spirals, etc.).

3. **Using a brush with coarse steel teeth.** This tool makes linear scratches and can be used for shading and highlighting.

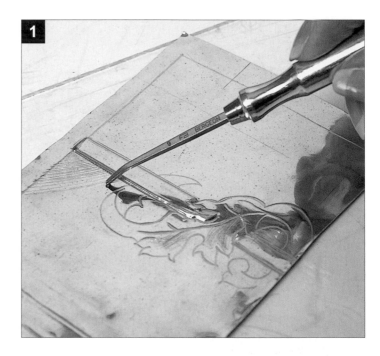

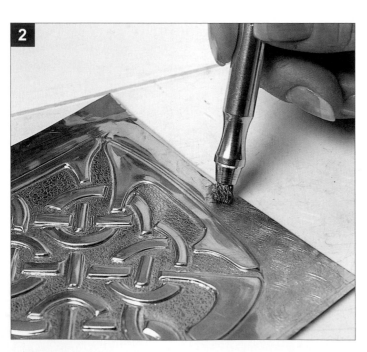

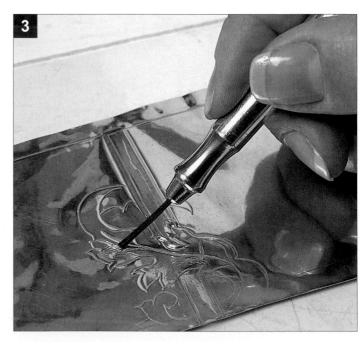

# Cutting Metal

You can cut metal with scissors, a craft knife, or specialized cutting tools. When cutting metal with a pointed tool, place it on the smooth side of a self-healing cutting mat and press along the area to be cut with the point of the tool. Depending on the hardness and thickness (gauge) of the metal, you may need to repeat the process several times.

1. **Cutting areas within designs.** Use a hardened steel dry point cutting tool to cut out areas of the embossed design. Cutouts allow the project surface to show through the cut openings and add interest to designs. Create the cutouts after the embossing is complete.

2. **Cutting metal around designs.** You can also use the hardened steel dry point tool to cut away the metal around a design to create an embossed metal cutout. The cutting is done when all the embossing is complete. The cutout can, for example, be glued to a surface.

3. **Cutting with scissors.** Decorative edge scissors can be used to cut designs along the straight edges on metal pieces.

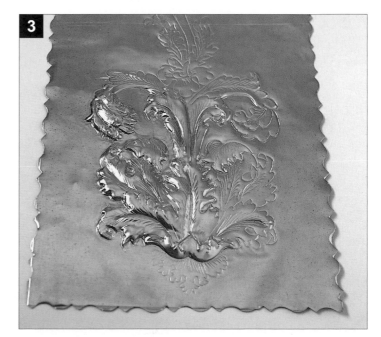

# Finishing

1. **Using decorating wheels.** Decorating wheels can be used to add finishing touches to the design. Here, rolling a decorating wheel between rows of embossed linework *(perfiles)* creates lines of dots.

2. **Wrapping an edge.** When an embossed panel is used to cover an entire surface, such as a drawer front or a frame, wrapping the metal around the edge creates a clean, finished look. After bending the metal, use the flat edge of a deerfoot tip hard plastic tool to burnish the edge. You can leave the metal smooth or add texture.

3. **Texturing the wrapped edge.** A decorating wheel can be used to create a design on a metal-wrapped edge. Here, a decorating wheel is used to create a fluted edge.

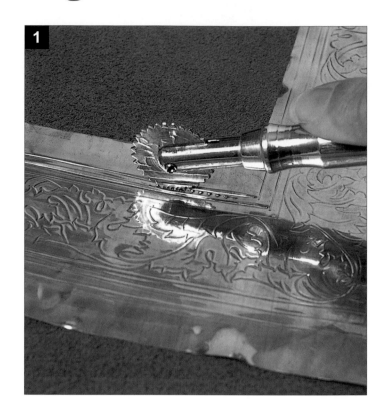

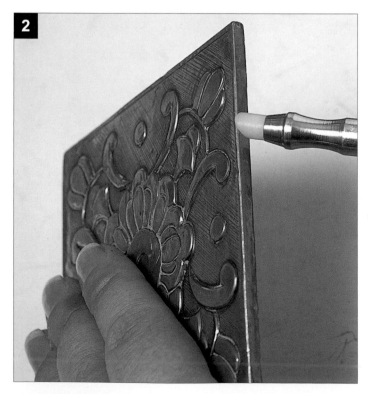

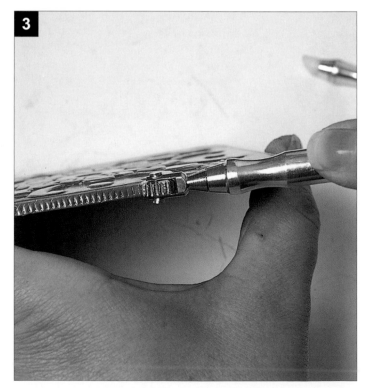

4. **Making a textured border.** Here, a decorating wheel is pushed along a turned edge to create a textured border. This border gives a decorative division to the textured embossed top and the flattened side.

5. **Protecting with lacquer.** Choose a lacquer intended for use on metal. Apply it before adding color such as alcohol-based inks as the lacquer can lift or remove the color.

6. **Antiquing.** You can also tint all or part of an embossed design with oil-based antiquing.

7. **Heating with a flame.** You can achieve interesting effects on copper by heating the metal with a flame, such as that of a craft torch, cigarette lighter, or a fireplace lighter. CAUTION: Take extra care when working with an open flame. Because copper is an excellent conductor of heat, **do not** hold the copper with your hands - use pliers instead so you won't burn your fingers.

# Adding Mother-of-Pearl Accents

Mother-of-pearl cutouts make colorful, shimmering accents on embossed metal projects. This photo sequence shows how to add mother-of-pearl accents, step by step, and includes an interesting technique that makes embossed lines look like rope. The Butterfly with Mother-of-Pearl Accents project, *pictured on opposite page* is used as an example.

## SUPPLIES

*In addition to metal, tools, and miscellaneous supplies for embossing, you'll need:*

**Mother-of-pearl** - This thin sheet comes with an attached adhesive backing. Find it in crafts stores.

**Sharp scissors**, for cutting the mother of pearl sheet.

**A pencil**, for marking the traced pattern lines.

## PROCEDURE

1. **Emboss.** After transferring the pattern, turn over the metal so the back side is up. Working over a suede piece, use the curved side of a refiner tool to emboss all the lines of the design.
2. **Refine.** Remove the suede and place the metal, front side up, on the acrylic glass. Press the curved edge of the refiner tool along the outside edges of the embossed lines to refine them.

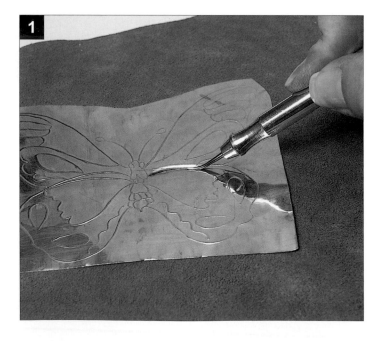

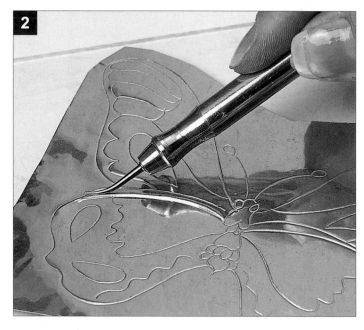

*Continued on page 44*

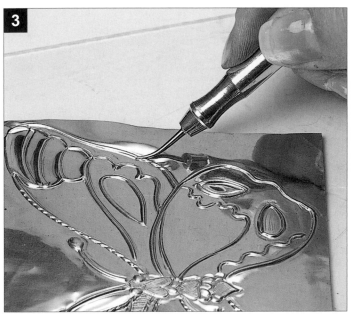

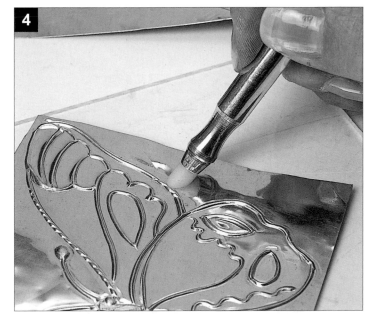

*Adding Mother-of-Pearl Accents, continued*

3. **Emboss for the look of rope.** Working on the front side, use the refiner tool to press parallel slanted lines into the embossed linework. The slanted lines mimic the look of twisted rope.

4. **Refine the edges.** Still working on the front, use the flat edge of a deerfoot-tip hard plastic tool to clean up along the edges of the design. Continue to emboss and refine until the design is complete. Using the photo as a guide, add texture to some of the flat areas of the design.

5. **Transfer the patterns.** Place the mother-of-pearl sheet face down on your work surface. Position the pattern on the mother of pearl. Use a stylus to transfer the patterns for the cutouts to the adhesive backing. (The stylus will create indentations in the backing paper.) Trace over the stylus lines with a pencil to make them easier to see while cutting.

6. **Cut out the pieces.** Cut out the mother-of-pearl pieces with scissors.

7. **Place the pieces.** Working one cutout at a time, remove the backing paper and place the mother-of-pearl cutouts on the embossed metal piece. ❏

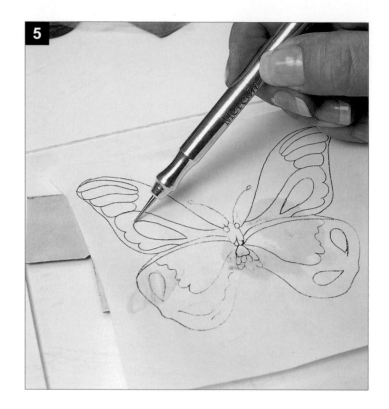

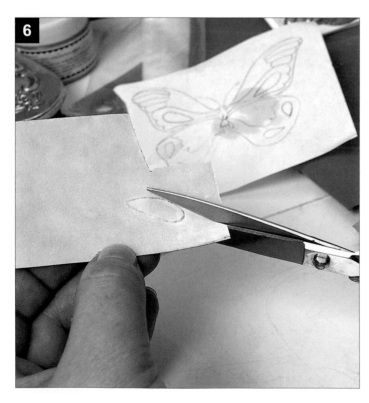

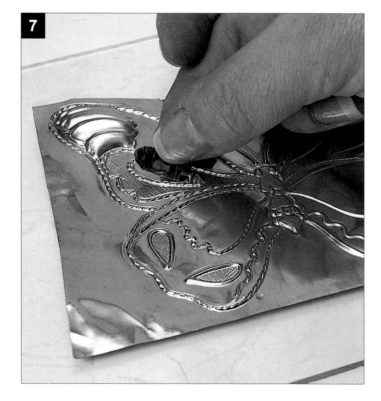

# PATTERN FOR BUTTERFLY

Pictured on page 43

# Adding Cabochon Gems

Cabochon gems are another way to add color and dimension to embossed metal designs. Use flat-backed gems of any size and shape. Semi-precious stones add a touch of elegance and authenticity to your designs. After the embossing is complete, cabochons are placed in holes cut from the metal and secured from the back with tape. You could use a punch to make the hole, but because cabochons can vary in size and shape, it's a good idea to use the particular gem you're planning to insert as a pattern for cutting the hole. This is much like making a bezel used in jewelry making techniques. This photo sequence shows how to add cabochons.

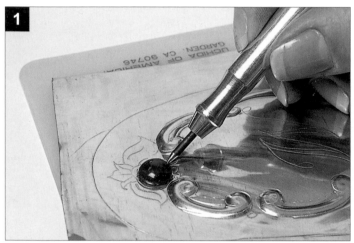

1. **Position the cabochon and begin the cutting.** Place cabochon on front side of the metal in the area of the design where you intend it to be. Trace around the cabochon, using a hardened steel dry point cutting tool to cut a hole the exact size and shape of the cabochon.

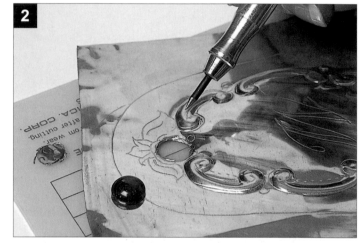

2. **Complete the cutting.** Remove the cabochon and set aside. Remove the metal cutout. If you didn't cut all the way through the metal, go over the outline again with the cutting tool to free the cutout.

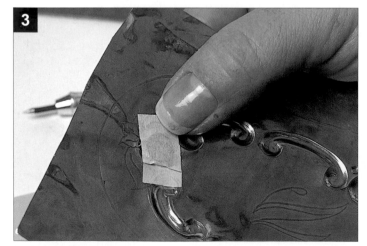

3. **Insert the gem.** Insert the cabochon into the cutout hole from the back of the metal piece. Place a piece of masking tape across the back to hold the cabochon securely in place.

4. **Smooth the opening.** Working over a cutting mat on the front of the metal piece, use the pointed tip of a hard plastic tool to smooth the metal around the opening and press it securely against the gem. ❑

# Repairing a Tear in Metal

Sometimes, no matter how careful you are, you may unintentionally tear the metal as you emboss. Don't despair! It's possible to repair the tear with a piece of self-adhesive metal tape. This photo sequence shows how.

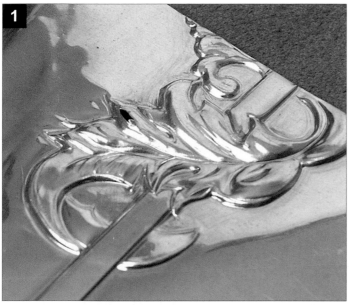

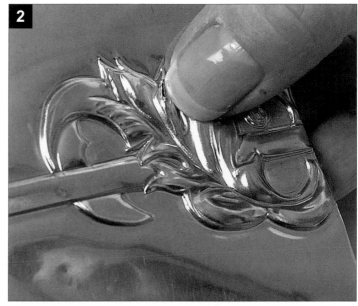

1. **Locate the hole.** Notice the tear in the metal in the scroll area of the design.

2. **Move the metal.** Use your thumbnail to push the edges of the tear together to minimize the hole as much as possible.

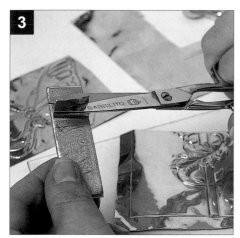

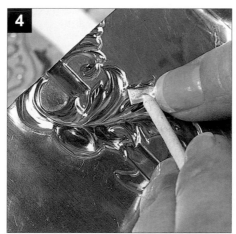

3. **Cut the tape.** Use scissors to cut a piece of self-adhesive metal tape big enough to cover the hole.

4. **Apply the tape.** Working on the back side of the embossed metal piece, press the metal tape over the hole to cover it. Hold it in place with your thumb and lightly press with a paper stump.

5. **Burnish.** When the tape is in place and adhered, burnish from the back with a paper stump. ❑

# Gluing a Metal Cutout

Embossed metal cutouts can be used to embellish all kinds of surfaces, including wood, ceramics, glass, and candles. The cutouts are light in weight and can be bent to fit curves. The glue you use depends on the surface to which you are adhering your embossed metal project. On wooden surfaces, use a heavy duty glue, strong rubber cement, or double-sided adhesive paper. For projects on paper or card stock (usually these are smaller projects), use adhesive paper, hot glue, double-sided tape, self-adhesive dots, or rubber cement.

These photos show how to attach an embossed cutout to a candle using rubber cement.

*TIP: When attaching metal to candles, you can also use small nails or pins.*

1. **Apply the glue.** Use a craft stick to spread it on the back of the embossed cutout.

2. **Position and press.** Position the cutout on the surface and press to attach. Let dry. ❏

## PATTERN FOR DECORATED CANDLE

# Using a Stamp as a Pattern

You can use a rubber or foam stamp as a pattern for an embossed metal design. Transferring the design is so simple - you just ink the stamp with washable ink and press it to the metal. That's it! You can also stamp the design onto tracing paper and use it as a regular pattern. This will allow you to reduce or enlarge the pattern. This photo sequence shows how, using the Copper Front Scrapbook, *pictured right, on opposite page,* as an example. Also pictured on opposite page are a fish and a grape design stamp that has been embossed to use on greeting cards.

1. **Stamp.** Stamp the design on the front of the metal piece, using washable ink.
2. **Trace.** Place the metal piece on the suede, front side up. Use the pointed end of a hard plastic tool or a round end stylus to trace the design and make impressions in the metal.
3. **Wipe.** Use a damp cloth to wipe the ink from the metal.
4. **Emboss.** Working on the back side of the piece and on the suede, use the ball end of a cup and ball tool or the double ball tool to emboss the design. Choose the tool that fits the size of the design.
5. **Define.** Turn piece to front. Working on the acrylic glass, define the lines of the design, using the pointed end of the hard plastic tool around the edge of the embossing.
6. **Add details.** Turn the metal so the back side is up and place on the suede. Use a refiner to add details. Here, the center vein of a leaf is embossed with the curved side of the refiner.

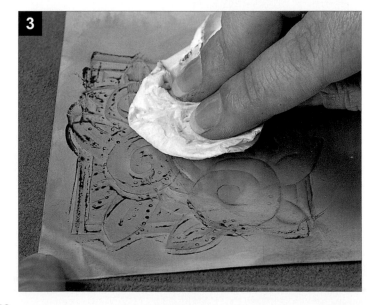

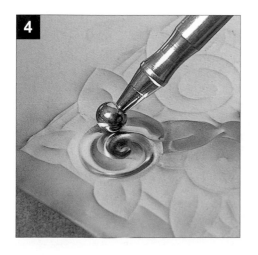

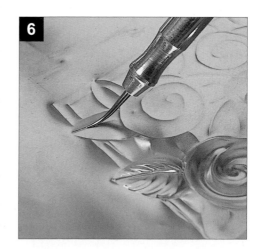

*Using a Stamp as a Pattern, continued*

7. **Add dimension with a cup and ball.** Continuing to work on the back side, use the ball end of a cup and ball tool to give dimension to the leaf.

8. **Add dimension with a refiner.** Still on the back of the metal piece, a refiner is used to add dimension and details to a leaf.

9. **Define.** On the front of the piece, you can see the results of the embossing. Working on the acrylic glass, the pointed hard plastic tool adds definition to the edge of the embossing.

10. **Add texture.** Add surface texture on the flat areas around the embossing by etching the metal, using the pointed end of the refiner tool. Here, a checkerboard design is used.

11. **Embellish the border.** Pull a decorating wheel along the straight edge of the design to embellish the border and add additional surface design. This is done on the front of the metal piece, working on suede for a deeper texture.

12. **Apply patina.** For an aged look, apply patina to the copper with a cotton ball when the embossing is complete. (Here, for demonstration purposes, this photo shows patina being applied to an incomplete design.)

13. **Wipe.** Use a soft cloth to wipe the patina from the raised areas of the design and polish the piece. You can leave as much or as little patina on the piece as you like.

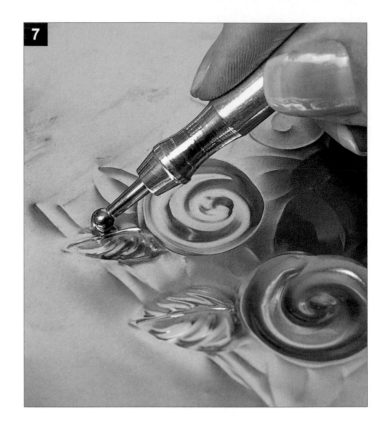

*Using a Stamp as a Pattern, continued*

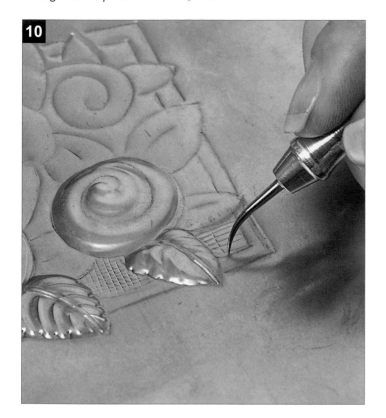

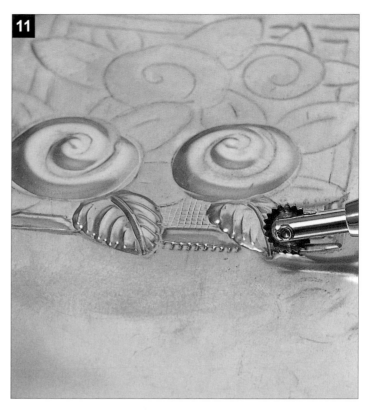

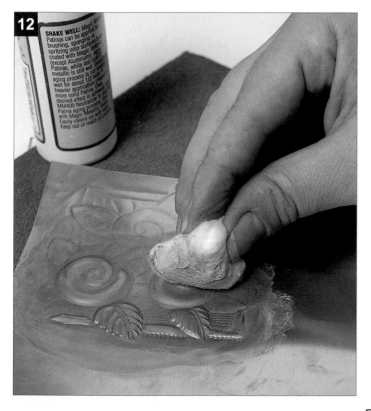

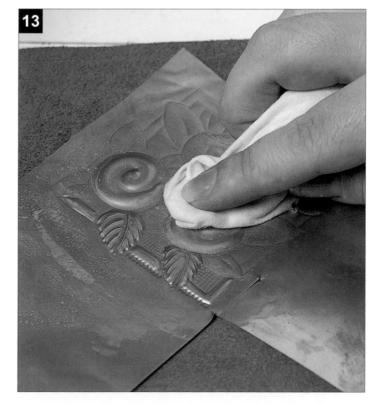

# Using a Stencil as a Pattern

Stencils are another source of patterns for embossed metal designs. Metal stencils or thick plastic stencils - kind used for paper embossing - work best. The stencil is kept under the metal as you emboss so it guides the tools as you work. This bee design that was used as an example is shown made into a pin and also glued to the front of a greeting card. Both are pictured on opposite page.

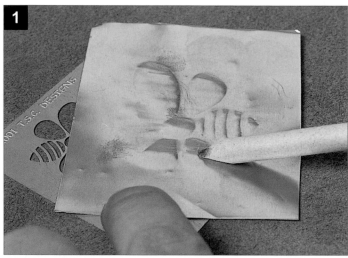

1. **Rub.** Place the suede piece on your work surface. Place the stencil on top of the suede. Place the metal piece on top of stencil. Rub the metal piece with a paper stump to impress the stencil design into metal.

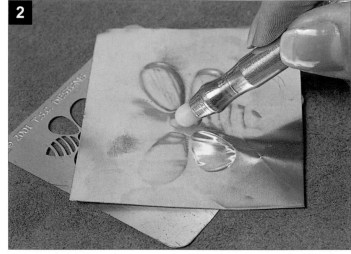

2. **Begin embossing.** With stencil still in place under the metal, use the round end of a hard plastic tool to emboss the design. Here, it's used on the bee's rounded wings and body.

3. **Continue embossing.** Use the pointed end of the hard plastic tool to emboss other smaller parts of the design, keeping the stencil in place. Here, stripes on the bee's body are embossed.

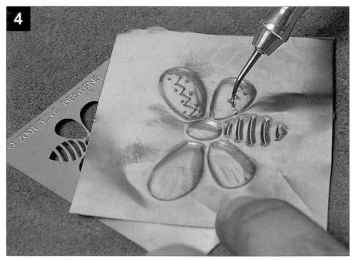

4. **Embellish.** Use the pointed end of the refiner tool to embellish a fanciful pattern on the wings. Again, the stencil is still in place.

*Using a Stencil as a Pattern, continued*

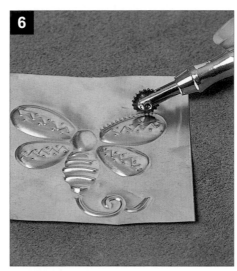

5. **Add details.** Remove the stencil. Use the pointed end of a hard plastic tool to add other design details, such as a flight line for the bee, working on the back side of the metal.

6. **Use a wheel.** Turn over the metal piece. On the front, use a decorating wheel to add additional surface design. Here, a wheel is used around the edges of the wings.

7. **Add colors.** When the design is complete, including the borders and background texture, use transparent paints and inks to add color to the metal.

These two pieces were created using the same stencil as a pattern. To make the Oval Bee Pin, *pictured at left above,* an embossed piece was mounted on a thin wooden base with a pin back. For the Colored Bee Card, *pictured at right above,* an embossed panel was colored with ink and mounted on a handmade layered paper card.

# Using Plastic Molds

Plastic molds are another source of designs for embossing. Use them to create borders around embossed motifs or for making embossed panels for cards, candles, or other surfaces. The photos that follow show how to make an embossed panel.

1. **Begin embossing.** Position a metal piece that's been cut to the desired size on top of the plastic mold. Use a paper stump to push the metal to create impressions from the mold.

2. **Deepen and enhance.** With the metal still in place on the mold, use a hard plastic tool to further deepen and enhance the embossing.

# Embossing Projects

The beauty and versatility of metal embossing is evident in this
next section. The projects show how embossing can be used to enhance and
decorate a variety of surfaces, including tabletop accessories (such as boxes,
trays, and napkin holders), frames for pictures and mirrors, wall pieces, and
traditional religious icons. You'll also see how to use embossing to embellish
scrapbook pages, cards, and candles.

Along with the project photos and descriptions, you'll find a tools list for
each project and patterns for the designs

# "Iniciales" Monogrammed Chest

This tiny chest is completely covered with embossed panels. Cut the metal panels before embossing. After embossing glue them to the chest with rubber cement. A geometric design with diagonal lines is used for the base; the panel on the top has space for initials and tiny lines in two patterns embellishing the background. A patina is applied before the design is colored. The monogram area is enhanced with a coat of Betun de Judea, which imparts a golden finish.

You can use computer fonts as sources for monogram letters - just print out your selected letters to size and use them as a pattern.

**Tools for This Project:**
Stylus, dry point cutter, refiner, small paper stump, small cup and ball tool

## PATTERN

SIDES

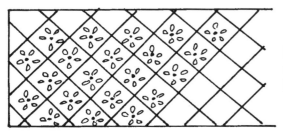

Repeat around box sides

TOP

# Magnificent Chest of Drawers

All the larger flat surfaces of this wooden jewelry chest are covered with embossed metal panels - the top, sides, curved back panel, and drawer fronts. The drawer embossed panels on the drawer fronts wrap around the edges of the drawers; the rest of the panels have embossed borders made with a wheel. After the panels were decorated, they were glued to the chest with rubber cement.

The drawer pulls were removed from the small wooden chest of drawers and all the wood, including the drawer pulls, was painted with gold paint. The embossed panels have cutouts for the drawer pulls. After the panels were glued in place, the drawer pulls were replaced.

The patterns appear on the following pages.

**Tools for This Project:**
Stylus, refiner, "large dot" decorating wheel, paper stump, microwheel, medium cup and ball, large cup and ball, pointed hard plastic tool, deerfoot hard plastic tool

# MAGNIFICENT CHEST OF DRAWERS
## PATTERN

Pictured on page 59

Actual Size

Actual Size

Sides – Enlarge 135%
for Actual Size

61

# Metal Lacework Tray

The floor of this wooden tray is covered with an embossed metal piece with a central design. Repeated motifs from the central design form a band on each end of the tray. A smaller repeated motif forms a border on all four sides. The leaf shapes were cut from the piece after the embossing using a dry point cutter. The cutout leaf shapes allow the wood of the tray to show through. The metal piece can be glued to the tray using rubber cement applied to the back of the metal piece. A piece of glass or hard plastic can be placed on top of the metal work to protect it so that the tray can be used.

The pattern appears on the following pages.

**Tools for This Project:**
Dry point cutter, stylus, refiner, small paper stump, small cup and ball tool

# METAL LACEWORK TRAY
## PATTERN

Pictured on page 62 & 63

Enlarge to 135% for Actual Size

# Ornamented Box

This box design has a base covered with embossed panels and an embossed inset panel on the top surrounded by a wooden frame. The sides of the frame are enhanced with embossed cutouts that create a decorative border. The background design on the base - short columns of closely spaced lines - provides a basket weave effect. The box was painted with red acrylic craft paint and antiqued with dark brown antiquing. The cutout pieces were glued to the box with rubber cement

**Tools for This Project:**
Dry point cutting tool, stylus, refiner, paper stump, hard plastic embossing tools of various sizes, "horizontal" decorating wheel, "horizontal wide" decorating wheel

## PATTERN

# Colorful Reliefwork Box

To create a stained glass effect, parts of embossed designs can be highlighted with inks or transparent paints. Deep jewel tones were chosen to complement the base color of this painted wooden box. The panel is a simple design made up of embossed outlines or "perfiles", curlicues, lines, and dots.

**Tools for This Project:**
Paper stump, small cup and ball, medium cup and ball, large cup and ball, hard plastic refiner tool, deerfoot hard plastic tool, refiner

# Madonna & Child Icon

The Madonna and Child is a traditional subject for religious Icons (panel paintings of holy subjects). At one time the faces would have been hand painted; this icon uses a Byzantine-style art print for the faces that was decoupaged to the wood surface on which the embossed panel was mounted. (Many makers of decoupage prints include religious prints; find them where decoupage papers are sold.)

One of the motifs from the frame was chosen and repeated to create the background; the space around the background motifs was filled in with freehand squiggles. The crowns for the two figures are embossed and cut out separately, then filled with filler paste and glued in place on the figures.

**Tools for This Project:**
Refiner, extra small cup and ball, small cup and ball, medium cup and ball, hard plastic refiner tool, deerfoot refiner tool, "big dots" decorating wheel, paper stump, dry point cutting tool, microwheel

Enlarge 165% for Actual Size

# Guarding the
# Silverware Box

This rectangular leather-covered hinged-top box would look great on a sideboard, where it could be used to store any number of things, including silver flatware. Embossed corner decorations, which are nearly but not quite symmetrical, are glued to opposite corners.

**Tools for This Project:**
Extra small cup and ball, refiner, chisel point hard plastic tool, rounded tip hard plastic tool, paper stump, dry point cutter.

# Celtic Design Box

Enlarge
140% for
Actual Size

The Celtic knot design embossed on the panel that tops this box was created using the technique for "High Level Flat Designs." (See the Basic Techniques section to learn this technique.) Tiny crosshatched lines, etched freehand with a microwheel, create a textured background that holds the patina in the crevices. A "dots" decorating wheel was used to make a beaded border around the edge.

**Tools for This Project:**
Refiner, microwheel, paper stump, pointed hard plastic tool, deerfoot hard plastic tool, "small dots" decorating wheel.

# Bejeweled Treasure Chest

See the following pages for the descriptions, tools used, and patterns for this project.

# Bejeweled Treasure Chest

Pictured on page 75

This wooden chest is covered with embossed metal panels. The metal panels were cut to fit the box before embossing. After embossing, adding patina, and polishing, the panels were glued to the wooden box.

The embossing was created using the high level flat relief technique (see "High Level Flat Designs" in the Basic Techniques section.) Some of the areas inside the flat bands were etched into a checkerboard pattern and scratched with a stylus. This was done from the front. Other areas have embossed lines that create the checkerboard design. The lines were embossed from the back with the refiner tool. Then the lines were refined on both sides with the same tool.

Purple cabochons in two sizes embellish the design. See section, "Adding Cabochon Gems" in the Basic Techniques for technique details.

**Tools for This Project:**
Dry point cutter, stylus, refiner, hard plastic embossing tools of various sizes, deerfoot hard plastic embossing tool, paper stump

Top

Slanted Front

Front

# Repoussé Poppy Plaque

A wooden plate with a painted rim becomes a frame for a round metal piece with an embossed poppy design. After the poppy panel was embossed, filled, and glued to the center area of the painted plate, an embossed and cutout butterfly with mother-of-pearl accents was added to the plaque. Only the center body part of the butterfly is attached so that the wings are dimensional and the butterfly looks as though he has alighted on the stem of the poppy. Small squiggles and fine lines create a finely textured background for the bold, smoothly embossed floral design.

**Tools for This Project:**
Dry point cutter, stylus, refiner, hard plastic embossing tools of various sizes, deerfoot hard plastic embossing tool, paper stump

Pattern for Butterfly can be found on page 82.

# Butterflies Shadow Box

Three embossed butterflies with mother-of-pearl accents arranged on a black fabric background within a shadow box make a dramatic wall piece. Each butterfly is made from a different pattern, and the mother of pearl accents on each butterfly's insets are a different color. See section "Adding Mother-of-Pearl Accents" in Basic Techniques for technique of adding the mother of pearl. Crosshatched lines (both bold and fine) and fine squiggles add texture to flat and embossed areas and create contrast with flat, untextured areas and rounded embossed details. The middle butterfly has the "twisted rope" technique explained in the section on "Adding Mother-of-Pearl Accents" in the Basic Techniques.

**Tools for This Project:**
Hard plastic refiner tool, hard plastic deerfoot tool, medium cup and ball, refiner, dry point tool, paper stump, hard plastic chisel tip tool, hard plastic half sphere tool

Additional patterns on page 82.

# BUTTERFLIES SHADOW BOX
## PATTERNS

# Tasseled Bookmark

An antiqued embossed panel with a squiggle background is an elegant addition to a black bookmark. A hole in the embossed panel lines up with the hole in the bookmark base. A white silken tassel is threaded through both holes.

**Tools for This Project:**
Dry point cutter, refiner, stylus, chisel-tip hard plastic tool, rounded tip hard plastic tool, small paper stump

# "Servilletero" Napkin Holder

This embossed napkin holder makes an elegant tabletop accessory. The central motif includes a cutout section that resembles a leaded glass window. A piece of mother-of-pearl sheet, taped behind the cutout area, gives the look of stained glass. A heavily textured background is enhanced by the application of a patina that gives an aged look.

TIP: If you want to cover the edges of your napkin holder with metal, be sure to allow for wrapping when deciding how big to cut the metal sheet.

**Tools for This Project:**
Dry point cutter, stylus, refiner, "big dot" decorating wheel, hard plastic embossing tools of various sizes. The "points" decorating wheel can be used to do a heavy textured background.

# Embossed Corners Frame

Embossed metal pieces are a great way to dress up picture frames. This one is leather. The embossed cutouts are simply glued to the purchased frame with rubber cement. Embossed pieces can be cutouts like the ones pictured, *opposite,* or they can wrap around the corners of the frame. Frames with wide, flat surfaces work best. You can use one, two, or four embossed pieces on a frame.

**Tools for This Project:**
Small cup and ball, refiner, paper stump, double ball tool, hard plastic refiner tool, deerfoot tip hard plastic tool, dry point cutter

# Illumination Decorated Candle

Metal embossing is a beautiful, safe way to decorate pillar candles. This candle, personalized with initials, was designed for a child's First Communion.

The tall candle, which is 2" in diameter, sits on a plain silver base and has a sleeve of embossed silver. The sleeve is wrapped around the candle, overlapped slightly at back of candle, and attached with four short straight pins or brads.

**Tools for This Project:**
Stylus, refiner, dry point cutter, "star" or "small dots" decorating wheel, deerfoot tip hard plastic embossing tool, pointed hard plastic embossing tool, brass brush, small cup and ball tool, paper stump

# Religious Ceremony Candle & Base

A silver sleeve wraps around a 3" diameter candle. The center motif is a religious symbol, but a monogram would also work in this area. The sleeve is wrapped around the candle, overlapped slightly at back of candle, and attached with four short straight pins or brads. The base, pictured below, is a circle of embossed pewter.

**Tools for This Project:**
Stylus, paper stump, refiner, dry point cutter, "diagonal" decorating wheel, "big dots" decorating wheel, pointed plastic refiner tool.

TOP

90

# Frame It Beautifully

An embossed metal frame gives a wonderful old world look to a vintage photograph. A single cabochon embellishes the embossed motif at the top. A piece of 1/4" thick bass wood was cut to the shape of the pattern. The metal design wraps around the sides of the wood. The metal is attached to the wood with rubber cement.

**Tools for This Project:**
Stylus, dry point cutter, refiner, various sizes of hard plastic embossing tools, double ball tool, small cup and ball tool, paper stump

# Flora Frame

The elaborate floral motifs of this rectangular frame are the perfect complement for a formal photograph. The star wheel was used to make the small dots around the opening and the perimeter of the frame. Freehand squiggles fill the background, adding texture.

**Tools for This Project:**
Stylus, dry point cutter, "star" decorating wheel, long brass brush (for texturing), refiner, microwheel, paper stump, medium cup and ball tool, large cup and ball tool, hard plastic refiner tool, deerfoot tip hard plastic tool

# "Joyero" Jewelry Box

Gorgeous blue-toned mother-of-pearl accents highlight the floral design embossed on the top of the lid of this square box. A wooden box is entirely wrapped in embossed metal. The panels are measures and cut before embossing. See the "Finishing" section in Basic Techniques for more information on how to cover a surface.

The same background texture, made with a wheel on the top, is also used on the side panels of the box. See the section, "Adding Mother-of-Pearl Accents" in the Basic Techniques for details on how to add the mother of pearl to the design. The panels are glued to the box with rubber cement.

**Tools for This Project:**
Refiner, stylus, small paper stump, hard plastic refiner tool, deerfoot tip hard plastic tool, "points" decorating wheel

# Personalized Leather Album

This medallion design can be used to create an elaborate emblem with a flat center area for embossed initials like the one that decorates the photo album, *opposite*. Or, with the center area cut away, the design could be used to create a frame for a photo or to decorate a surface that would show through the opening.

The center area of the metal cutout is "puffed" using a wooden thumb while the piece is held in the palm of the hand. See the section "Embossing Curving Designs" in Basic Techniques for instructions and photos on how to "puff" a design.

**Tools for This Project:**
Stylus, refiner, wooden thumb, "star" decorating wheel, cup and ball tools, various sizes of hard plastic tools, paper stump

Enlarge Pattern 140% for Actual Size

# Cross with Cabochons

Christian religious symbols and icons are traditional subjects for embossed metal pieces. Here, five blue cabochons accent an ornamented cross. An applied patina adds to the antique look; the freehand-squiggled background provides texture to the surface where the patina can settle. The side metal wrapping was textured with a brass brush. See section on "Surface Texturing" in Basic Techniques for more information.

A 3/4" thick piece of pine was cut by the pattern outline. Pieces of metal were measured and cut to wrap around the sides of the piece and glued to the wood with rubber cement. Joints were planned so that they occur in the indented areas of the outline. For photos and details on attaching cabochons, see section "Adding Cabochon Gems" in Basic Techniques.

**Tools & Supplies for This Project:**
Refiner, medium large cup and ball, hard plastic refiner tool, deerfoot tip hard plastic tool, paper stump, brass brush, four 15mm blue cabochons, one 20mm blue cabochon.

Enlarge 110% for Actual Size

# Frame Easels

These covered wooden easels are just the thing for holding a frame, a plate, or a tray upright at just the right angle for display. Two 3/4" thick pieces of wood were cut by the pattern outline. All the surfaces are covered with the metal. Metal pieces were measured and cut before embossing, and attached with rubber cement after embossing. The metal panels for the edges were given a simple cross hatch linework pattern done with a stylus or refiner from the front with the metal piece on suede for cushioning. The background of the design panels was done with a refiner. See section "Surface Texturing" in Basic Techniques for more information on adding background textures. Also see "Finishing" in Basic Techniques for more information on covering a surface with metal pieces.

**Tools for This Project:**
Stylus, refiner, paper stump, hard plastic refiner tool, deerfoot tip hard plastic tool, chisel tip hard plastic tool, half sphere hard plastic tool

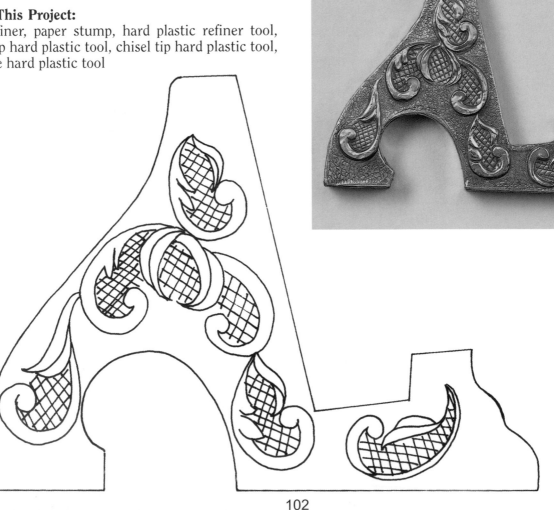

# Scrolls Covered Box

Embossed metal completely covers this ornate box. Backgrounds of fine lines on the top of the lid and the upper areas of the base create a pleasing contrast with areas that are left smooth. A decorating wheel is used for the border separating the two areas on the lid. The metal panels were measured and cut before embossing; then attached with rubber cement after embossing.

See section "Surface Texturing" in Basic Techniques for more information on adding background textures. Also see "Finishing" in Basic Techniques for more information on covering a surface with metal pieces.

**Tools for This Project:**
Stylus, "horizontal" decorating wheel, paper stump, refiner, extra large cup and ball, hard plastic refiner tool, deerfoot tip hard plastic tool

Repeat design
around sides of box

# Bordered in Beauty Mirror

A 12" x 16" oval mirror with a stained wooden frame is the beginning point of this project. The series of embossed metal motifs that surround the frame of this mirror are reminiscent of a necklace or a belt. The metal designs were done in sections of four. Small sapphire crystals are inset in holes on the sections that join the groups of motifs and act as spacers. (Add beads as you would cabochons - see "Adding Cabochon Gems" in the Basic Techniques section.)

See "Cutting Metal" in Basic Techniques for more information on how to cut out the metal pieces. The cut edges of the pieces were finished with a dash decorating wheel.

**Tools & Supplies for This Project:**
Dry point cutter, stylus, refiner, double ball tool, paper stump, chisel tip hard plastic tool, rounded tip hard plastic tool, deerfoot tip hard plastic tool, "dash" decorating wheel (for edges of cutout), 2mm crystals for spacers (as many as needed)

Enlarge pattern 200% for Actual Size

# Mirror Elegance

The embossed metal piece covers the front of this shaped edge oval mirror frame, allowing just the wooden edge to show. The frame was cut from 3/4" thick plywood, following the pattern outline. The edges of the frame were beveled and a mirror cut to fit inside oval. The plaque was stained a dark brown.

The background is covered with random squiggles done with a stylus, refiner, or a microwheel for a traditional look. Three lapis-look cabochons in different sizes embellish the design. For photos and details on attaching cabochons, see section "Adding Cabochon Gems" in Basic Techniques. After the embossing was complete, the piece was glued to the plaque front with rubber cement.

**Tools & Supplies for This Project:**
Stylus, refiner, big double ball tool, cup and ball tool, paper stumps, pointed hard plastic refiner tool, deerfoot tip hard plastic tool, microwheel, wooden thumb (to puff the shell), "star" decorating wheel, one 20x30mm oval cabochon, one 15mm round cabochon, two 7mm round cabochons.

Enlarge pattern 200% for Actual Size

# "Buena Mano" Card Box

This ornate box is just the right size for two decks of playing cards. It makes a beautiful addition to your game table and would be a lovely gift for card-playing friends. A dark patina enhances the dimensionality of the embossed design.

**Tools for This Project:**
Stylus, refiner, wooden thumb, paper stumps, various sizes of hard plastic embossing tools, double ball

# Key Safe

The door and surrounding frame of this wooden key cabinet take on a formal, important look with the addition of embossed panels. Mother-of-pearl accents decorate the curved top panel, the sides, and the door. An interesting effect is created by using a decorating wheel to make intersecting lines. The small diamond-shaped areas within the lines are carefully cut away, and the design areas are backed with mother-of-pearl cutouts that show through the thin embossed lines.

**Tools for This Project:**
Stylus, refiner, wooden thumb, paper stumps, various sizes of hard plastic embossing tools, dry point cutter, medium and large cup and balls, mother of pearl sheet (self-adhesive)

Enlarge pattern
145% for
Actual Size

TOP

SIDE PANELS (reverse & repeat on opposite side)

*Patterns continued on page 114*

# KEY SAFE
Enlarge Pattern 145% for Actual Size

Instructions on page 112

# A Gift of Elegance

An embossed medallion, attached to the top of a jar lid, turns the jar into an attractive storage canister or festive packaging for a gift of candy, cookies, or other treats. The circular design is cut out and glued to the lid. If you're recycling a jar, it's easy to spray paint the lid to create a plain background for the embossing.

**Tools for This Project:**
Stylus, refiner, paper stumps, various sizes of hard plastic embossing tools, big cup and ball tool.

115

# Vines & Twines Vase

Like a beautiful lacy collar, a round embossed cutout surrounds the opening of this red vase. After embossing, cutting, and filling with paste is complete, the metal piece is gently fitted to the shape of the vase, and attached with rubber cement.

**Tools for This Project:**
Stylus, dry point cutter, refiner, paper stumps, various sizes of hard plastic embossing tools

Enlarge pattern to 135% for Actual Size

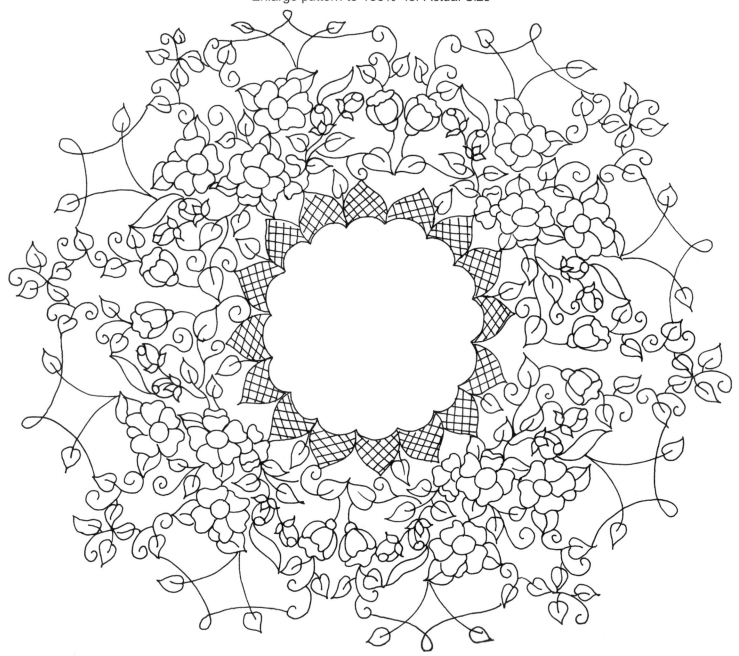

# Precious Memories
# Scrapbook Pages

Embossed metal accents add dimension and shine to scrapbook pages. Use them for borders, decorative accents for photos and printed images, cutouts, and labels to give your pages a custom look.

The **Fashion Page** has layers of decorative papers, vintage newspaper and catalogue prints, and a sepia-toned photo trimmed with deckle-edge scissors accented with embossed aluminum bands created with plastic molds.

On the **My Angel Page**, decorative papers and mesh provide the background for an angel motif rubber stamp. The stamped image on green vellum has an embossed halo and wings - the rubber stamp was used as the pattern for the embossing. Metal cutouts, an embossed label, and skeleton leaves complete the page.

The **Grandma Page** includes layers of paper and vintage photos, an embossed initial on a metal-rimmed tag, embossed name and date labels, and embossed decorative accents.

**Tools for Fashion Page**
Plastic molds, paper stump, chisel tip hard plastic tool, rounded tip hard plastic tool, extra small cup and ball tool, stylus, herringbone decorative wheel

**Tools for My Angel Page**
Paper stump, chisel tip hard plastic tool, rounded tip hard plastic tool, refiner, saw teeth brush or brass brush (for textures), decorative wheels (squares, Morse code, big wheel, triple, herringbone)

**Tools for Grandma Page**
Decorative wheels (Morse code, big, star), refiner, hard plastic refiner, deerfoot hard plastic tool, paper stump, small cup and ball, large cup and ball

*Pictured at right, top to bottom:*
Fashion Page, My Angel Page, Grandma Page

# Ornamented Accordion Card

This two-sided accordion-fold collage has embossed copper pieces on one side and embossed pewter and golden aluminum pieces on the other. Layers of paper and mesh form the foundation and create layered backgrounds for the metal.

On the copper side, stencils were used to create the inside medallion and the leaf on the cover. A plastic mold was used for the rectangle. The corner triangles and the two long strips were decorated with wheels. Green patina gives an aged look to the Mayan medallion. A lighter was used to alter the color of other pieces.

On the other side, three square golden aluminum charms were created with a brass stencil. The cutout motif was created with a rubber stamp. The pewter corner motif was embossed with decorating wheels. The rectangular piece has a dotted border (made with a wheel) and circles made with a cup and ball tool.

**Tools for This Project:**
*Copper Side* - Decorating wheels (dash, points, triple, horizontal, star, diagonal with gap, Morse code, big wheel), refiner, paper stump, small cup and ball, large cup and ball, chisel point hard plastic tool, rounded tip hard plastic tool
*Pewter and Golden Aluminum Side* - Paper stump, small cup and ball, medium large cup and ball, refiner, chisel point hard plastic tool, rounded tip hard plastic tool, decorating wheels (horizontal, diagonal, star, big wheel, points, narrow)

# Two Arts
# Box and Frame

Embossed metal cutouts are a great way to add three-dimensional accents to decorative painting projects. On both the box and the frame, *pictured opposite page,* cutout embossed flowers and vines were glued in place after the folk art-style painting was complete. An embossed border surrounds the photo on the inner edge of the frame.

**Tools for These Projects:**
Medium and large cup and ball, refiner, paper stump, big decorating wheel, dry point cutter

Pattern at Right – Box Sides
Repeat around Box

*Additional patterns on pages 124, 125*

Box Sides

# TWO ARTS BOX & FRAME

Enlarge pattern 118% for Actual Size

# Metric Conversion Chart

## Inches to Millimeters and Centimeters

| Inches | MM | CM | Inches | MM | CM |
|--------|----|----|--------|----|----|
| 1/8 | 3 | .3 | 2 | 51 | 5.1 |
| 1/4 | 6 | .6 | 3 | 76 | 7.6 |
| 3/8 | 10 | 1.0 | 4 | 102 | 10.2 |
| 1/2 | 13 | 1.3 | 5 | 127 | 12.7 |
| 5/8 | 16 | 1.6 | 6 | 152 | 15.2 |
| 3/4 | 19 | 1.9 | 7 | 178 | 17.8 |
| 7/8 | 22 | 2.2 | 8 | 203 | 20.3 |
| 1 | 25 | 2.5 | 9 | 229 | 22.9 |
| 1-1/4 | 32 | 3.2 | 10 | 254 | 25.4 |
| 1-1/2 | 38 | 3.8 | 11 | 279 | 27.9 |
| 1-3/4 | 44 | 4.4 | 12 | 305 | 30.5 |

## Yards to Meters

| Yards | Meters | Yards | Meters |
|-------|--------|-------|--------|
| 1/8 | .11 | 3 | 2.74 |
| 1/4 | .23 | 4 | 3.66 |
| 3/8 | .34 | 5 | 4.57 |
| 1/2 | .46 | 6 | 5.49 |
| 5/8 | .57 | 7 | 6.40 |
| 3/4 | .69 | 8 | 7.32 |
| 7/8 | .80 | 9 | 8.23 |
| 1 | .91 | 10 | 9.14 |
| 2 | 1.83 | | |

# Index

*Continued on next page*